Filling Fajitas

Quick Weeknight Fajita Recipes that Anyone Would Enjoy Eating

BY - Zoe Moore

Copyright 2022 by Zoe Moore

Copyright Notes

I've spent a lifetime in the kitchen, and all the knowledge I've accumulated from that hasn't come without its fair share of burns and disasters. Fortunately, I'm a lot wiser from it all and am now in a place where I can share my knowledge and skills with you. However, that doesn't mean anyone can use my content for any purpose they please. This book has been copyrighted as a way to protect my story, knowledge, and recipes, so I can continue sharing them with others into the future.

Do not make any print or electronic reproductions, sell, re-publish, or distribute this book in parts or as a whole unless you have express written consent from me or my team.

This is a condensed version of the copyright license, but it's everything you need to know in a nutshell. Please help protect my life's work and all the burns and melted spatulas I have accumulated in order to publish this book.

Table of Contents

Introduction 5

   (1) Chili Fajita 7

   (2) Chicken Fajita with Bay Leaf 9

   (3) Chicken Fajita with Herb Lemon Mix 11

   (4) Beef Mix Fajita 13

   (5) Mexican-Style Fajita 15

   (6) Shrimp Fajita 17

   (7) Baked Chicken Fajita 19

   (8) Halibut Fajita 21

   (9) Beef and Shrimp Fajita 23

   (10) Salmon Fish Fajita 25

   (11) Fajita Burger Patty 27

   (12) Lemon Shrimp Fajita 29

   (13) Shell Fajita Pasta 31

   (14) Corn Chicken Fajita 33

   (15) Baked Bell Pepper Fajita 35

(16) Chicken Apricot Fajita 37

(17) Fajita Sandwiches 39

(18) Cheesy Chicken Fajita 41

(19) Fajita Filled Chicken 43

(20) Peanut Chicken Mix Fajita 45

(21) Chicken Full Fajita Filled 47

(22) Balsamic Onion Simple Fajita 49

(23) Full Vegetables Fajita 51

(24) Vegetable Fajita with Chicken Scampi 53

(25) Cabbage Fajita Wrap 55

(26) Butterfly Pasta Mix Fajita 57

(27) Mix Fajita with Black Olives 59

(28) Spaghetti with Fajita 61

(29) Big Tomatoes Fajita 63

(30) Rigatoni Fajita 65

About the Author 68

Author's Afterthoughts 69

Introduction

Regardless of why you eat so many fajitas, you need new recipes in your weeknight rotation ASAP. That's why you're here isn't it? We're not sure anyone could ever get tired of this delicious dish, but why take any chances? To spice things up a little, we're bringing you a wide selection of fajitas using all of your favorite ingredients! Tomatoes, bell peppers, onion, shrimp, fish, beef, mushrooms, you name it!

If you can think of it, we've got it. Even if we don't, by the time you're done with our cookbook, you'll be ready to start experimenting with your own fajita recipes like a pro. We recommend going through your fridge and freezer to check what ingredients we can work with and then selecting a recipe from there. There's no need to go shopping for more food when you've got little bits of different leftovers! So, chop it all up and get ready to enter a new phase of meal prepping in your life.

These fajitas are cheap, easy, quick, and delicious. What more could you ask for? Get off the couch right now and start flipping through this book because we're already heating some oil in a pan to get started. If you're not sure where to begin, we recommend the peanut-chicken mix fajitas but it's totally up to you. Let's get started!

xxxxxxxxxxxxxxxxxxxxxxxxxxxxxxxxxxxxxxxxxx

(1) Chili Fajita

Try this amazing spicy chili fajita at dinner. You will love its sizzling taste!

Cooking Time: Twenty minutes

Yield: Two to three

List of Ingredients:

- Two tbsp. of dill
- Two sliced lemons
- Two sliced green bell pepper
- Two tbsp. of red pepper flakes
- Two lb. of sliced chicken
- Two tbsp. of pepper
- Two sliced red bell pepper
- Two sliced onions
- Two tbsp. of oil
- Two tbsp. of red chili powder

xxxxxxxxxxxxxxxxxxxxxxxxxxxxxxxxxxxxxxxx

How to Cook:

Heat oil in a pan.

Stir pepper with chicken. Mix it constantly and cook for about ten minutes.

Then, add the green bell pepper, dill, red pepper flakes, and red chili powder.

Mix it well and add sliced onions with red bell pepper.

While mixing, cook it for twenty minutes.

Serve the sizzling chili fajita at dinner and enjoy.

(2) Chicken Fajita with Bay Leaf

The best recipe to try for dinner as it contains vitamins, copper, and proteins!

Cooking Time: Forty-five minutes

Yield: Two to three

List of Ingredients:

- One tbsp. of turmeric powder
- Half cup of milk
- Two tbsp. of vegetable oil
- One bay leaf
- One tbsp. of garlic powder
- Half can of tomato paste
- One tbsp. of coriander powder
- Tow onions
- One cup of yogurt
- Two tbsp. of cinnamon powder
- One lb. boneless chicken
- Two tbsp. of ginger powder

xxxxxxxxxxxxxxxxxxxxxxxxxxxxxxxxxxxxxxx

How to Cook:

Add vegetable oil to a heated pan. Then, add the boneless chicken, onion, and garlic powder.

Allow it to cook for about ten minutes, and then add a half can of tomato paste. Add half a tsp. of ginger powder, coriander, cinnamon, and turmeric powder and mix it well.

Mix milk and yogurt to make a thick mixture.

Then, add the mixture and cover it to mix well.

As chicken fajita gets ready, garnish it with bay leaf pieces and enjoy.

(3) Chicken Fajita with Herb Lemon Mix

Since lemons are a rich source of vitamin B6 and vitamin C, this herb lemon mix chicken fajita will give you a full vitamin and protein diet!

Cooking Time: Twenty-five minutes

Yield: Two to three

List of Ingredients:

- One pinch of oregano
- Pepper and salt as per taste
- Two cubed chicken breast
- Two cups of parsley
- Two cups of herbs
- One lemon
- One tbsp. of oil

xxxxxxxxxxxxxxxxxxxxxxxxxxxxxxxxxxxxxxxxx

How to Cook:

Rinse the chicken and pour lemon over it until it absorbs it entirely.

Cook oregano in a heated pan with oil. Take the chicken breast and cut it into cubes. Let the chicken cook for a while.

Cook the chicken for about twenty minutes, and then add the herbs.

As chicken cooks, add pepper and salt as per taste. Garnish with parsley and serve.

(4) Beef Mix Fajita

An amazing combo of fajita with beef which is also rich in proteins for your health!

Cooking Time: Thirty minutes

Yield: Two to three

List of Ingredients:

- Two tbsp. of oil
- Two tbsp. of oregano
- One lb. of sliced beef
- Two tbsp. of red chilies
- Two sliced red bell pepper
- Two tbsp. of minced garlic
- Two sliced green bell pepper

xxxxxxxxxxxxxxxxxxxxxxxxxxxxxxxxxxxxxxxx

How to Cook:

Let the oil heat in a pan.

Then, add beef and garlic to it.

For twenty minutes, cook it. Add the green bell pepper and red bell pepper, as the beef looks soft and tender.

For another ten minutes, cook it and keep mixing for two more minutes.

Serve the beef mix fajita and enjoy it with your family and friends.

(5) Mexican-Style Fajita

Mexican-style fajita gives you a different taste of fajita!

Cooking Time: Thirty minutes

Yield: Two to three

List of Ingredients:

- Sixteen ounces spaghetti
- One tbsp. of taco seasoning mix
- Half equally chopped onion
- One can of diced tomatoes
- One pound of ground turkey
- One twenty-four ounces spaghetti jar sauce
- Salt as per taste
- One tbsp. of olive oil
- One tsp. of chili powder
- Ground black pepper as per taste
- One small-seeded and minced jalapeno pepper

xxxxxxxxxxxxxxxxxxxxxxxxxxxxxxxxxxxxxxxxx

How to Cook:

Take a pan and add oil to it.

Cook the pasta in another pot. Set it aside after it gets cooked.

Add the jalapeno, chili powder, pepper, turkey, salt, and onion to the pan.

For about twenty minutes, cook the mixture.

Add the sauce and tomato can.

Cook for more ten minutes.

Stir the taco seasoning with the pasta and serve.

(6) Shrimp Fajita

Stay healthy by eating shrimp fajita that contains copper, iodine, and vitamin B12!

Cooking Time: Twenty minutes

Yield: Two to three

List of Ingredients:

- Two tbsp. of cornstarch
- One tsp. of honey
- Four tbsp. of water
- ¼ tsp. of vegetable oil
- One tbsp. of soy sauce
- Two onions
- Two tbsp. of ketchup
- One lb. of shrimps with tails removed
- Half tsp. of ginger powder
- Two minced garlic cloves
- One sliced green bell pepper

xxxxxxxxxxxxxxxxxxxxxxxxxxxxxxxxxxxxxxxx

How to Cook:

In a bowl, mix cornstarch with ketchup and water. Combine it well, and add the soy sauce, honey, ginger powder, and green bell pepper.

Set it aside for some time. Cook the onions in a pan heated with oil.

Mix the shrimps in the pan with onions. Then, add the minced garlic cloves in it and sauce prepared before. Cook for another ten minutes.

Serve the delicious shrimp fajita and enjoy.

(7) Baked Chicken Fajita

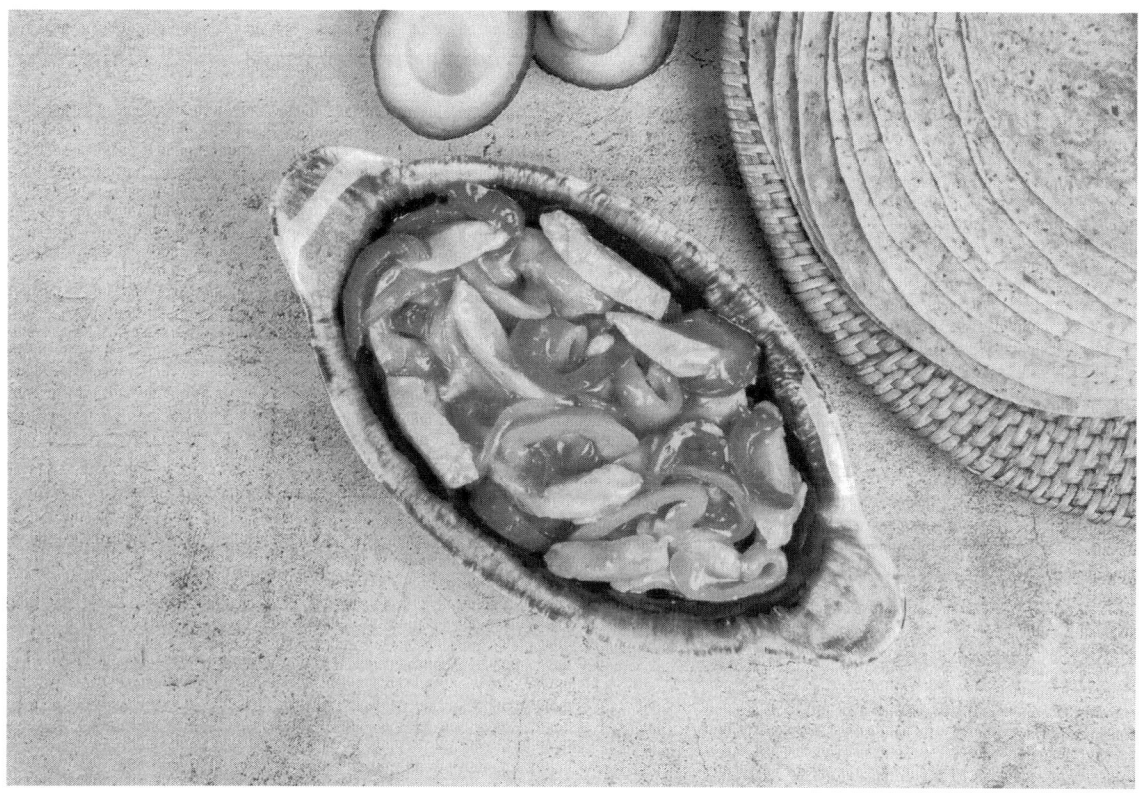

Want to try something different tonight? Well-baked chicken fajita is the one that will give you a colorful yet different taste!

Cooking Time: Twenty minutes

Yield: Two to three

List of Ingredients:

- Pepper and salt as per taste
- Two sliced onions
- One lb. of baked chicken slices
- Two garlic
- Two sliced yellow pepper
- Two tbsp. of turmeric powder
- Two tbsp. of oil
- Two sliced red bell pepper

xxxxxxxxxxxxxxxxxxxxxxxxxxxxxxxxxxxxxxxxxx

How to Cook:

Mix the baked chicken slices in oil within a pan.

Let it heat, and then add the turmeric powder, pepper, garlic, and salt.

Mix it well and cook for about two minutes.

Add the green bell pepper, sliced onions, and green bell pepper.

Combine it well and cook for two more minutes.

Serve the baked chicken fajita and enjoy.

(8) Halibut Fajita

Halibut fajita is rich in protein, vitamin B12, potassium, and selenium!

Cooking Time: Forty minutes

Yield: Two to three

List of Ingredients:

- Two tbsp. of garlic powder
- Two tbsp. of paprika
- One tbsp. of lemon juice
- Six halibut fillets
- Two green bell pepper
- One tbsp. of onion powder
- Two tbsp. of lemon pepper
- One tbsp. of dill
- One cup of parsley
- Two red bell pepper

xxxxxxxxxxxxxxxxxxxxxxxxxxxxxxxxxxxxxxxx

How to Cook:

Prepare a baking dish at 375 F. preheat the oven. Let the halibut fillets dry after washing them. You will fill the halibut fillets with a mixture.

Add the lemon pepper, onions, salt, dill, garlic powder, and paprika with parsley. Stir well and add lemon juice to it.

For about twenty minutes, bake it wrapped in foil.

Serve the halibut fajita when it is ready and enjoy.

(9) Beef and Shrimp Fajita

Try this wild mixture of beef and shrimp for dinner tonight!

Cooking Time: Twenty minutes

Yield: Two to three

List of Ingredients:

- Two tbsp. of oil
- Two sliced tomatoes
- Two lb. of shrimps
- Two tbsp. of red chili powder
- Two sliced green bell pepper
- Pepper and salt as per taste
- One lb. sliced beef
- Two sliced onions

xxxxxxxxxxxxxxxxxxxxxxxxxxxxxxxxxxxxxxxxx

How to Cook:

Take a pan and add oil to it.

Combine the beef and shrimp and, on high flame, cook it for about twenty minutes.

Then, add the red chili powder, pepper, green bell pepper, tomatoes, salt, and onions.

For about thirty minutes, cook the mixture.

Serve the beef and shrimp fajita and enjoy dinner with your friends.

(10) Salmon Fish Fajita

Salmon fish fajita is a complete meal that provides potassium, vitamin D, proteins, and selenium for you to stay healthy!

Cooking Time: Fifty minutes

Yield: Two to three

List of Ingredients:

- Two sliced onions
- One to two salmon
- Half cup of maple syrup
- Pepper and salt as per taste
- Two tbsp. of garlic powder
- Two sliced red bell pepper
- Two tbsp. of soy sauce

xxxxxxxxxxxxxxxxxxxxxxxxxxxxxxxxxxxxxxxxx

How to Cook:

Combine the soy sauce with maple syrup.

Add garlic powder, pepper, and salt to it. Stir it well and rinse the salmon pieces.

Then, add the red bell pepper and onion and cook for about two minutes.

At 350°F, preheat the oven and spread the paste on salmon. Bake the salmon for about twenty minutes in the oven and enjoy.

(11) Fajita Burger Patty

Are you feeling hungry? Try this best combo of fajita burger patty!

Cooking Time: Twenty minutes

Yield: Two to three

List of Ingredients:

- One burger patty
- Two tbsp. of soy sauce
- Two sliced onions
- One bun
- Guacamole for serving
- Two sliced green bell pepper
- Pepper and salt as per taste
- Two sliced red bell pepper
- Two tbsp. of oil

xxxxxxxxxxxxxxxxxxxxxxxxxxxxxxxxxxxxxxxx

How to Cook:

Prepare the burger patty beforehand.

Add the onion to a heated pan with oil.

Combine the red bell pepper and green bell pepper.

Add soy sauce with pepper and salt and cook it for about ten minutes.

Take a bun and place the prepared burger patty in it. Put the fajita filling over it.

Cover the bun, serve the fajita burger and enjoy.

(12) Lemon Shrimp Fajita

Need the energy to go through the day. Well, lemon shrimp fajita is rich in iron, fiber, and vitamins to give you strength!

Cooking Time: Thirty minutes

Yield: Two to three

List of Ingredients:

- Two cups of parsley
- Two sliced onions
- Two tbsp. of butter
- Two sliced orange bell pepper
- Two tbsp. of white wine
- Pepper and salt as per taste
- Two cups of lemon juice
- Two tbsp. of minced garlic cloves
- Two sliced red bell pepper
- One lb. cleaned shrimp

xxxxxxxxxxxxxxxxxxxxxxxxxxxxxxxxxxxxxxxx

How to Cook:

Add parsley with pepper and salt in a pan.

Combine it well and add white wine and minced garlic to it. Add shrimps to it and make a thick sauce.

Then, add the lemon juice, onions, and bell pepper. Cook it for another two minutes.

When the mixture is tender and cooked, serve and enjoy.

(13) Shell Fajita Pasta

This dish is one of the most desirable combinations of fajita with shell pasta. Try it, and you will remember its taste!

Cooking Time: Twenty minutes

Yield: Two to three

List of Ingredients:

- Two tbsp. of garlic paste
- Ketchup as per taste
- Two cups of boiled shell pasta
- Two tbsp. of ginger paste
- Two lb. of chopped chicken
- Pepper and salt as per taste
- Two cups of parsley
- Two tbsp. of oil
- Two sliced onions

xxxxxxxxxxxxxxxxxxxxxxxxxxxxxxxxxxxxxxxx

How to Cook:

Set aside the boiled shell pasta in a bowl.

Mix parsley in a pan with oil.

Then, add the ginger paste, chicken, and garlic paste and cook it for about ten minutes.

Stir in the pepper and salt with ketchup.

For about twenty minutes, cook the mixture.

Serve when shell fajita pasta gets ready and enjoy.

(14) Corn Chicken Fajita

Get enough magnesium, phosphorus, vitamin B6, and fiber from corn chicken fajita. You will surely love its taste!

Cooking Time: Forty minutes

Yield: Two to Three

List of Ingredients:

- Half cup of lemon juice
- Two lb. cubed chicken
- Pepper and salt as per taste
- Two tbsp. of oil
- Two cups of corn kernels
- Half cup of bell pepper
- Two minced onions
- Half cup of Jicama
- One cup of cilantro leaves

xxxxxxxxxxxxxxxxxxxxxxxxxxxxxxxxxxxxxxxxxx

How to Cook:

Heat a pan with oil on low heat.

Add jicama and bell pepper to a bowl. Combine it well with onions and corn by adding cilantro leaves and lemon juice.

Then, mix the pepper and salt with corn kernels.

Cook chicken in a pan for about ten minutes.

Add the mixture and cook again for about thirty minutes.

Serve when the corn chicken fajita is ready and enjoy.

(15) Baked Bell Pepper Fajita

If you don't like cooking, then make this baking recipe of bell pepper fajita. You will love its taste!

Cooking Time: Twenty minutes

Yield: Two to three

List of Ingredients:

- Two tbsp. of red chili pepper
- Two tbsp. of lemon juice
- Two sliced yellow bell pepper
- One lb. of cubed chicken
- Pepper and salt as per taste
- Two sliced onions

xxxxxxxxxxxxxxxxxxxxxxxxxxxxxxxxxxxxxxxx

How to Cook:

Prepare a baking dish with a foil cover, and at 350°F, preheat the oven.

Spread sliced onions and yellow bell pepper on the baking dish.

Then, sprinkle red chili pepper, pepper, and salt.

Lastly, add the cubed chicken, and for twenty minutes, bake it in the oven.

Serve the baked bell pepper fajita and enjoy it with your loved ones.

(16) Chicken Apricot Fajita

A meal full of vitamin C, fiber, potassium, protein, and copper that will fill your stomach!

Cooking Time: Fifty-five minutes

Yield: Two to three

List of Ingredients:

- Two cups of fresh thyme
- Two cups of chicken stock
- Four slices of bread
- Two tbsp. of oil
- Pepper and salt as per taste
- Two pounds of cubed chicken breast
- Two cups of cheese
- Two onions
- Two mashed apricot
- Two tbsp. of vinegar

xxxxxxxxxxxxxxxxxxxxxxxxxxxxxxxxxxxxxxxx

How to Cook:

Take a pan and heat oil in it.

Add pepper, salt to the chicken, and cook it in a pan. Cook the fresh thyme, onion, apricot, and chicken stock with vinegar.

For about twenty minutes, cook it.

Combine the mixture well as it gets ready pour it on chicken breast.

Allow it to melt after adding cheese to it.

On the bread slice, spread this prepared mixture and serve.

(17) Fajita Sandwiches

For sandwich lovers, this recipe is tasty and healthy. You will try it repeatedly!

Cooking Time: Twenty minutes

Yield: Two to three

List of Ingredients:

- Four slices of bread
- Pepper and salt as per taste
- Two chopped capsicums
- Two chopped onions
- Two cups of cheese
- One lb. of chopped chicken
- Two tbsp. of oil

xxxxxxxxxxxxxxxxxxxxxxxxxxxxxxxxxxxxxxxx

How to Cook:

Set aside the bread slices after grilling them.

Cook chicken for about two minutes in a pan with oil.

Then, add the pepper, onion, salt, and capsicum.

For about twenty minutes, cook the mixture.

As it gets cooked, add cheese to it.

Fill the bread slices with the prepared mixture and then grill them.

Serve the fajita sandwiches and enjoy with your friends.

(18) Cheesy Chicken Fajita

Cheese chicken fajita is highly nutritious as it contains vitamin A, protein, vitamin B12, and zinc, which is required by your body daily!

Cooking Time: Fifty minutes

Yield: Two to three

List of Ingredients:

- Two tbsp. of pesto
- Two cups of spinach
- Two tbsp. of oil
- Shredded cheese
- Two chicken breasts
- Two tbsp. of alfredo sauce
- Two garlic cloves

xxxxxxxxxxxxxxxxxxxxxxxxxxxxxxxxxxxxxxxxx

How to Cook:

Add oil to a pan. Cook the garlic cloves and then add the chicken breast in them as pieces.

Take another pan, add the alfredo sauce and spinach leaves and cook it. Also, boil the pesto pasta.

Spread cheese and let it melt as it gets cooked.

Serve when cheesy chicken fajita is ready and enjoy.

(19) Fajita Filled Chicken

You will love its moist and soft texture. Fajita-filled chicken is rich in calcium, so you must try it once!

Cooking Time: Thirty minutes

Yield: Two to three

List of Ingredients:

- Two tbsp. of garlic paste
- One tbsp. of lemon juice
- One cup of flour
- Two green bell peppers
- Two tbsp. of red pepper flakes
- One lb. minced chicken
- Two sliced onions
- Two red bell peppers
- Pepper and salt as per taste

xxxxxxxxxxxxxxxxxxxxxxxxxxxxxxxxxxxxxxx

How to Cook:

Take a bowl and add chicken to it.

Mix the pepper and salt with flour.

Then, add the lemon juice, red pepper flakes, and garlic paste.

Make a layer, and then add the green bell pepper, onion, and red bell pepper.

Just like a filling, roll it.

On a baking tray, place chicken patties, and at 350°F, heat the oven.

For about thirty minutes, bake it in the oven.

Serve when fajita chicken is ready and enjoy.

(20) Peanut Chicken Mix Fajita

It contains nuts, providing copper, potassium, iron, zinc, and calcium, good for maintaining your healthy body!

Cooking Time: Forty minutes

Yield: Two to three

List of Ingredients:

- Two tbsp. of oil
- Roasted peanuts
- Two minced garlic cloves
- Two tbsp. of cayenne pepper
- Broccoli
- One lb. sliced beef
- Two onions
- Two tbsp. of vinegar
- Two tbsp. of peanut butter
- Two tbsp. of soy sauce

xxxxxxxxxxxxxxxxxxxxxxxxxxxxxxxxxxxxxxxxxx

How to Cook:

Add oil in a pan separately—Cook garlic in the pan. Then, add the beef to the pan and cook it. Lastly, add the soy sauce and vinegar to it and cover it for some time.

Add the broccoli and cayenne pepper to it as you smell beef.

Add the peanut butter at the end and stir it with a spoon.

Serve as peanut chicken fajita gets ready and garnish it with roasted peanuts.

(21) Chicken Full Fajita Filled

This fajita is a complete meal of vitamins and proteins for you. You won't regret trying it!

Cooking Time: Thirty minutes

Yield: Two to three

List of Ingredients:

- Two tbsp. of red chili powder
- Two tbsp. of garlic paste
- One lb. chicken
- Two tbsp. of soy sauce
- Two chopped red bell pepper
- Pepper as per taste
- Two chopped green bell pepper

xxxxxxxxxxxxxxxxxxxxxxxxxxxxxxxxxxxxxxxx

How to Cook:

In a bowl, add the red chili powder to the chicken.

Then, coat the chicken with soy sauce and pepper.

Add green bell pepper, garlic paste, and red bell pepper to the chicken.

Prepare a baking tray, and at 350°F, preheat the oven.

For about twenty minutes, bake the chicken in the oven.

Serve when chicken fajita filled is ready and enjoy.

(22) Balsamic Onion Simple Fajita

A unique and delicious fajita combination rich in zinc, calcium, and magnesium, keeping you energized all day!

Cooking Time: Thirty minutes

Yield: Two to three

List of Ingredients:

- Two sliced red bell pepper
- Two cups of thyme
- One tbsp. of oregano
- Two tbsp. of garlic powder
- Two sliced yellow bell pepper
- Two tbsp. of oil
- Half tsp. of rosemary
- Pepper and salt as per taste
- Two tbsp. of chopped basil
- Two tbsp. of vinegar
- Two sliced onions
- Two sliced green bell pepper

xxxxxxxxxxxxxxxxxxxxxxxxxxxxxxxxxxxxxxx

How to Cook:

Heat oil in a pan and add garlic to it. Add all the bell peppers as the garlic turns light brown.

Add pepper and salt as per taste, and then add sliced onions to it. Combine it well after adding thyme to it.

Mix the rosemary and oregano too.

Allow it to cook for about twenty minutes and cover it. Serve as balsamic onion simple fajita gets ready and enjoy.

(23) Full Vegetables Fajita

A delightful fajita combination with vegetables that you can have with any meal!

Cooking Time: Thirty minutes

Yield: Two to three

List of Ingredients:

- Two tbsp. of soy sauce
- Sliced onions
- Two eggs
- Two cups of peas
- Two tbsp. of minced garlic cloves
- Half cup of sesame oil
- Two cups of water
- Two carrots

xxxxxxxxxxxxxxxxxxxxxxxxxxxxxxxxxxxxxx

How to Cook:

Add oil to a pan.

Add onions, peas, and carrots to a bowl.

Boil all the vegetables in water and cut them into small pieces before mixing them in the bowl.

Add the minced garlic and sesame oil to it.

Lastly, add soy sauce to it and microwave it for about ten minutes. Your vegetable fajita is ready.

(24) Vegetable Fajita with Chicken Scampi

A scrumptious meal that gives you enough zinc, sodium, protein, potassium, magnesium, and calcium to fulfill your daily nutrient needs!

Cooking Time: Thirty minutes

Yield: Two to three

List of Ingredients:

- Two crushed garlic cloves
- White sauce or white wine
- One lb. boneless chicken
- Half cup of lemon juice
- Pepper and salt as per taste
- Oregano
- Two cups of shredded cheese
- Half tbsp. of oil
- Two cups of parsley

xxxxxxxxxxxxxxxxxxxxxxxxxxxxxxxxxxxxxxxx

How to Cook:

Heat oil in a pan. Add the chicken and garlic to it. Allow it to cook for about ten minutes.

Add pepper and salt to it as per your taste. Spread the oregano pieces in the mixture and add lemon juice to it.

Take chicken out in a baking dish as it gets cooked and spread parsley and cheese on it. Then, add the white sauce or white wine as per your liking and bake it for about ten minutes at 325°F in the oven.

As chicken scampi with vegetable fajita gets ready, serve it with any side dish and enjoy.

(25) Cabbage Fajita Wrap

Most people prefer wraps due to their taste and convenience. Thus, you will love this cabbage fajita wrap for sure!

Cooking Time: Fifty minutes

Yield: Two to three

List of Ingredients:

- Two cups of cabbage
- Half cups of coconut flour
- Four eggs
- Two cups of radish
- ¼ cup of Psyllium husks
- Salt for taste

xxxxxxxxxxxxxxxxxxxxxxxxxxxxxxxxxxxxxxxxx

How to Cook:

Boil the eggs and then mash them.

Add Psyllium husks and salt with radish and cabbage. Combine it with coconut flour and fill in the Pita bread. Wrap the bread.

For about five minutes, put the wrap in the microwave. The cabbage fajita wrap is ready to eat.

You can eat this wrap with rice or any other side dish. You can make this wrap easily, even during hectic schedules.

(26) Butterfly Pasta Mix Fajita

One of the tastiest and most healthy meals to give you energy all day!

Cooking Time: Thirty minutes

Yield: Two to three

List of Ingredients:

- One lb. of chopped chicken
- One package of butterfly pasta
- Half pound of Italian sausage
- One tbsp. of dried basil
- Pepper and salt as per taste
- Two cans of tomato sauce
- One tbsp. of dried oregano
- Two bay leaves
- Half tsp. of garlic powder
- One tbsp. of Italian seasoning
- Two chopped red and green bell pepper

xxxxxxxxxxxxxxxxxxxxxxxxxxxxxxxxxxxxxxxxx

How to Cook:

1. Brown the sausages over medium flame in a large skillet. Strain it and set it aside.

2. On medium flame, set a large saucepan and add the garlic powder, Italian sausage, oregano, salt, basil, pepper, and garlic powder with tomato sauce, bay leaves, Italian seasoning, and diced tomatoes. Mix the mixture well.

With chicken, add the green and red bell peppers. For about twenty minutes, cook it.

Take another pot and boil the butterfly pasta. As pasta gets ready, mix both and serve.

(27) Mix Fajita with Black Olives

Delicious fajita combination for black olive lovers!

Cooking Time: Thirty minutes

Yield: Two to three

List of Ingredients:

- Two cups of beets slices
- Two chopped tomatoes
- Two cups of minced garlic
- Avocado oil for cooking
- Two cups of basil
- Two cups of black olives
- Two cups of minced parsley
- Two tbsp. of pumpkin pie sauce
- Pepper and salt as per taste

xxxxxxxxxxxxxxxxxxxxxxxxxxxxxxxxxxxxxxxxx

How to Cook:

Add the pumpkin sauce, oil, salt, parsley, pepper, garlic, and basil in a pan and combine it well.

As per your desire, you can add the beet slices.

Mix well with black olives and tomatoes.

For about thirty minutes, cook the mixture.

As the mixture gets ready, fill the pita bread and wrap it. Serve and enjoy.

(28) Spaghetti with Fajita

The most desirable combination that you will love once you try it!

Cooking Time: Thirty minutes

Yield: Two to three

List of Ingredients:

- Two tbsp. of freshly chopped parsley
- One minced garlic clove
- Pepper and salt as per taste
- One tbsp. of olive oil
- ¼ cup of dry white wine
- One finely sliced onion
- One pound spaghetti
- Eight diced bacon slices

xxxxxxxxxxxxxxxxxxxxxxxxxxxxxxxxxxxxxxx

How to Cook:

Take a pot and boil the spaghetti in it.

In a large skillet with oil, cook the bacon slices till they are crispy. Strain them with a paper towel.

Set aside the bacon and pour olive oil in the skillet. On medium flame, add the chopped onions too.

Cook for one minute after putting in minced garlic. If you are adding white wine, then cook for one more minute.

In a pan, add the spaghetti and bacon.

Add some olive oil if the mixture sticks while mixing it.

Garnish your fajita spaghetti with parsley and serve.

(29) Big Tomatoes Fajita

This fajita is a delicious and healthy meal to have at lunchtime!

Cooking Time: Thirty minutes

Yield: Two to three

List of Ingredients:

- Two minced garlic
- Two tomatoes
- One egg
- Two tbsp. of cumin powder
- One cup of all-purpose flour
- Two tbsp. of tomato paste
- One cauliflower
- One cup of mint leaves
- Salt as per taste
- Two tbsp. of oil

xxxxxxxxxxxxxxxxxxxxxxxxxxxxxxxxxxxxxxxxx

How to Cook:

Mix milk, minced garlic, cumin powder, and flour in a bowl and blend well.

Add boiled tomatoes and egg.

Take a baking tray and spread the mixture in it. At 350°F, preheat the oven.

For about twenty minutes, bake the mixture in the oven.

As big tomatoes fajita is ready, serve and enjoy.

(30) Rigatoni Fajita

Rigatoni fajita recipe is a delicious combo for your lunch!

Cooking Time: Twenty-five minutes

Yield: Two to three

List of Ingredients:

- Two sliced red bell pepper
- One pinch of dried chili flakes
- Two cups of dried rigatoni
- Three garlic cloves
- Two cups of parsley minced
- Two tsp. of dried oregano
- Four sausages
- Two cups of chopped tomatoes
- Two cups of cheddar cheese
- Two tbsp. of olive oil

xxxxxxxxxxxxxxxxxxxxxxxxxxxxxxxxxxxxxxxxxx

How to Cook:

At 395°F, preheat your oven, and add the garlic pieces mixed with grated cheddar.

In a bowl, add the sliced garlic clove with grated cheese, breadcrumbs, sprinkling oregano, and a pinch of salt and pepper. Mix it with some oil, so all ingredients are combined well.

Put sausages in an ovenproof dish and sprinkle some oil to coat them. Allow them to bake for ten minutes till they are cooked entirely.

Over medium flame, put some oil in a frying pan. Stir the oregano with chili flakes and sliced garlic. Combine well till garlic is colored. Tip in with the chopped tomatoes.

Add a pinch of salt, red bell pepper, pepper, and parsley to the mixture.

Boil the rigatoni separately and then mix it with the mixture. Serve and enjoy.

About the Author

From a young age, Zoe loved being in the kitchen! More specifically, her uncle's bakery. Despite not actually working there, she would sit on the working table and watch herself get covered in flour over the next couple of hours. She also watched closely as her uncle kneaded the dough, measured out ingredients, and even decorated cakes. Even though she never tried doing it herself, she could recite the steps to most of the baked goods sold like her favorite song.

It wasn't until her 16th birthday, though, that she realized just how much she wanted to dedicate her life to making desserts too. No matter how much Zoe's mom insisted on buying a beautiful cake from a local bakery for her Sweet 16 party, Zoe wouldn't budge. She wanted to make the cake herself, and she did. Even though it wasn't the prettiest of cakes, it tasted delicious! Her whole family still remembers the flavor combo to this day: pistachio and orange cake. From there, things only got better!

After graduating from culinary school, Zoe worked in some of the finest bakeries throughout Europe. She wanted to learn from the best. Eventually, however, she decided to go back home and start her own business in Chicago, near her friends and family. That business is now one of the nicest bakeries in the city, which she has run with the help of her best friend, Lola, since 2015

Author's Afterthoughts

Hi there!

This is me trying to thank you for supporting my writing by purchasing my cookbook. I can't begin to express how much it means to me! Even though I've been doing this for quite a while now, I still love to know that people enjoy making my recipes, and I like to thank them for it personally.

You see, without you, my job would be meaningless. A cook with no one to eat their food? A cookbook author with no one to read their book? I need you to love my work to be rewarding, so do you?

One of the biggest ways to thank you for supporting me is by asking what you like or dislike most about my books. Are the recipes easy to follow? Do you think I should write more baking books, or what would you like to see more of? I will get to your suggestions for new books and improvements soon, ready to use them for my next book — so don't be shy!

THANK YOU.

ZOE MOORE

Printed in Great Britain
by Amazon